Grandmas GONE WILD

COURAGE
BOOKS

AN IMPRINT OF RUNNING PRESS
PHILADELPHIA • LONDON

9 8 7 6 5 4 3 2 1
Digit on the right indicates the number of this printing.

Library of Congress Control Number: 2005903189

ISBN-13: 978-0-7624-2639-3
ISBN-10: 0-7624-2639-X

Designed by Corinda Cook
Photography researched by Susan Oyama
Edited by Michael Tomolonis

This book may be ordered by mail from the publisher. *But try your bookstore first!*

Published by Courage Books, an imprint of
Running Press Book Publishers
125 South Twenty-second Street
Philadelphia, Pennsylvania 19103-4399

Visit us on the web!
www.runningpress.com

Contents

Introduction

Most of us are conditioned to expect certain behavior from grandmothers. We expect a smile of delight and fresh baked cookies when we arrive at their doors, a warm embrace before we leave to drive home or a comforting anecdote when we have a bad day. We have come to accept these cozy images of grandmothers alongside many other beliefs. Grandmas are wise. Grandmas are forgiving. Grandmas are caring. But what about grandmas gone wild?

Grandmas gone wild are our young-hearted conspirators. They wear odd clothing and keep us on our toes with pranks and jokes. These women unabashedly speak their minds to strangers while we pretend not to feel uncomfortable. They wander around the backyard and spy on their neighbors. They are playful, defiant, fun-loving, and hysterical sources of joy. For grandmas gone wild, youth is simply a state of mind.

Gathered here are words on aging, fun, strength, family, and remembering from well-known people who have used age-old insights to describe the behavior of these beloved members of society. Their thought-provoking sentiments seem oddly appropriate here. The photographs prove that traditional thoughts about grandmothers can sometimes ring true in unexpected ways when grandmas go wild!

On Aging

My grandson was visiting one day when he asked,
"Gramma, do you know how you and God are alike?"
I mentally polished my halo while I asked,
"No, how are we alike?"
"You're both old," he replied.

Author Unknown

Those of us who
are old can afford to
live dangerously.
We have less to lose.

Maggie Kuhn (1905–1990)

American civic activist

A passionate interest in what you do is the secret of enjoying life, perhaps the secret of a long life, whether it is helping old people or children or making cheese or growing earthworms.

Julia Child (1912–2004)

American chef

Beauty is accepting what you are, who you are, and how old you are. Ugliness is when you try to be something else.

Sophia Loren, b. 1934

Italian actress

I LOOK FORWARD TO GROWING OLD AND WISE AND AUDACIOUS.

Glenda Jackson, b. 1937

English actress

I don't want to *fight* old age, but I'm not about to invite it to live in, either. I want a nice symbiotic relationship with it, where we are totally unaware of each other.

Betty White, b. 1924

American actress

If you pretend old age is not going to happen, it will fall right on you.

Julia Child (1912–2004)

American chef

20

Perhaps one has to be very old before one learns to be amused rather than shocked.

Pearl S. Buck (1892–1973)

American writer

Judging by the world's press

I am the only grandmother in the world.

Marlene Dietrich (1901–1992)

American actress

If you don't have wrinkles, you haven't laughed enough.

Phyllis Diller, b. 1917

American comedian

What is it about a grandparent
that is so lovely?
I'd like to say that grandparents are
God's gifts to children.
And if they can but see, hear,
and feel what these people have to give,
they can mature at a fast rate.

Bill Cosby, b. 1937

American comedian

Grandchildren don't make a man feel old; it's the knowledge that he's married to a grandmother.

G. Norman Collie (1859–1942)

British scientist

On Fun

Time and trouble will tame an advanced young woman,
but an advanced old woman is uncontrollable by any earthly force.

Dorothy Sayers (1893–1957)

English writer

Well! Some people talk of morality, and some of religion, but give me a little snug property.

Maria Edgeworth (1767–1849)

English writer

Life is a big thing, it's got size, and you shouldn't be applying your passion to puny things. Life is a struggle for the human heart and the human spirit, a struggle between good and bad for good and bad.

Peggy Noonan, b. 1950

American writer

When grandparents enter the door, discipline flies out the window.

Ogden Nash (1902–1971)

American poet

Grandmother, family-proud and so of house, with hob black-leaded, glistening like a raven's wings and brass like gold untarnished.

Brian Harris

20th century American author

Grandmas . . . can shed the yoke of responsibility, relax, and enjoy their grandchildren in a way that was not possible when they were raising their own children. And they can glow in the realization that here is their seed of life that will harvest generations to come.

Erma Bombeck (1927–1996)

American writer

On Strength

Nothing can help us face the unknown future
with more courage and optimism
than remembering the glory moments,
and everybody has a few of them.

Eda LeShan

20th-century American writer

There is a fountain of youth: it is your mind, your talents, the creativity you bring to your life and the lives of the people you love. When you learn to tap this source, you will have truly defeated age.

Sophia Loren, b. 1934

Italian actress

My grandmother was a very tough woman. She buried three husbands and two of them were just napping.

Rita Rudner, b. 1956

American actress, comedian, author

You have to stay in shape. My grandmother, she started walking five miles a day when she was 60. She's 97 today and we don't know where the hell she is.

Ellen DeGeneres, b. 1958

American comedian

She was a buxom grandmother noted for her detective stories, who gazed mournfully at the camera as if deploring either the bloodiness of her craft or the size of her advance.

P. D. James, b. 1920

English novelist

MY GRANDMOTHER IS OVER EIGHTY
AND STILL DOESN'T NEED GLASSES.
DRINKS RIGHT OUT OF THE BOTTLE.

Henny Youngman (1906–1998)

American comedian

In the effort to give good and comforting answers to the young questioners whom we love,
we very often arrive at good and comforting answers for ourselves.

Ruth Goode

20th-century American writer

The purpose of living is to get

old enough to have something to say. . . .

M.F.K. Fisher (1908–1992)

American writer

On Family

If a tie is like kissing your sister,
losing is like kissing you grandmother with her teeth out.

George Brett, b. 1953

American baseball player

A house needs a grandma in it.

Louisa May Alcott (1832–1888)

American writer

Have children while your parents are still young enough to take care of them.

Rita Rudner, b. 1956

American actress, comedian, author

Nothing is more important to human happiness than to be part of a fractious, forgiving, warm, tightly knit family.

Marjorie Holmes

20th-century American writer

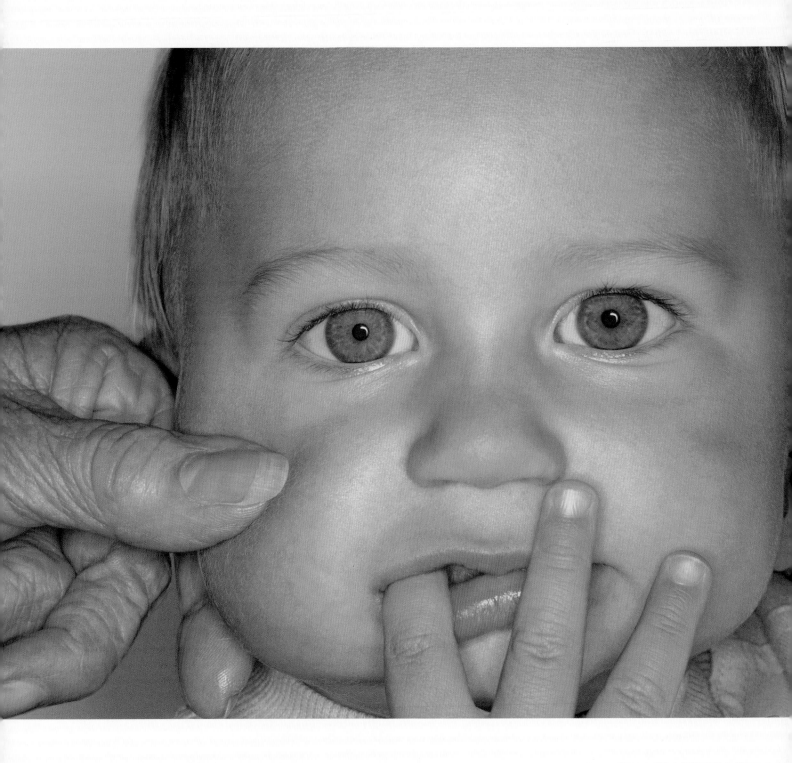

A grandmother corrects your grammar and wipes imaginary dirt from our cheeks.

Sara Spurrier (age 12)

English youngster

Having grandchildren is
the best of all possible worlds.
I don't have any
responsibility for them—
I just do all the fun stuff.

Author Unknown

Grandchildren provide us with some of our proudest occasions, some of our tenderest experiences, and, without question, some of our funniest moments.

Catharine Brandt

20th-century American writer

Grandma always made you feel she had been waiting to see just you all day and now the day was complete.

Mary DeMaree

20th-century American writer

Grandmother-grandchild relationships are simple.
Grandmas are short on criticism and long on love.

Author Unknown

Grandmothers don't have to do anything except be there . . . It is enough if they drive us to the market, where the pretend horse is, and have lots of dimes ready. Or if they take us for walks, they slow down past things like pretty leaves or caterpillars. They should never "Hurry up."

Patsy Gray (age 9)

American youngster

There are only two families in the world, my old grandmother used to say, the Haves and the Have-nots.

Miguel de Cervantes (1547–1616)

Spanish novelist

On Remembering

Do the young seek absolute truth?

Take me along, too.

After all, I might have earlier crossed this way,

and when you feel as quicksand,

I might feel as concrete, the path hardened by values

I learned when I passed before.

Pearl Bailey (1918–1990)

American actress and writer

That was one of the good things about getting old: you weren't perpetually in a hurry . . . There was time to stop and look, and, looking, to remember.

Rosamunde Pilcher

20th-century American writer

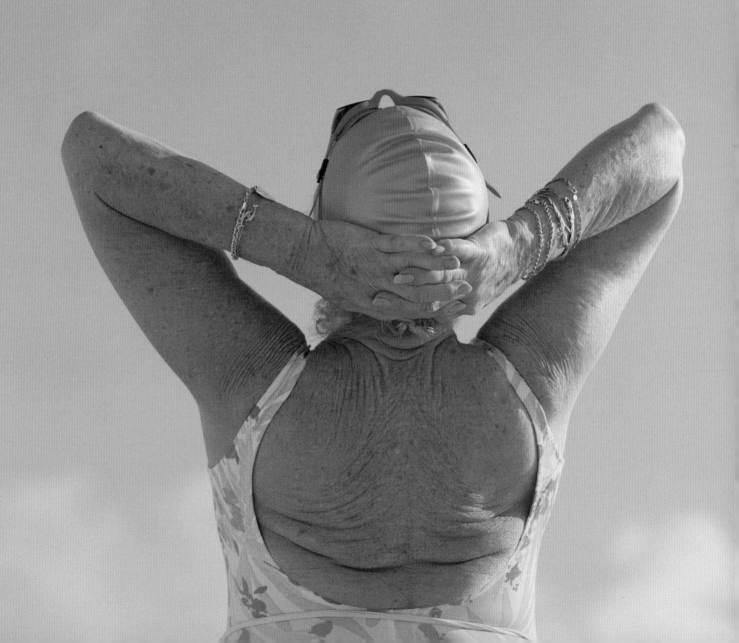

Things are new even at the age when we are supposed to have seen everything.

Louise Erdrich, b. 1954

American writer

I've had lots of kids come up

and ask for my autograph.

I've had a grandmother stop

me and ask me if I know

a good place to buy underwear.

Prince William, b. 1982

The Prince of Wales

Growing older frees you from all sorts of previous restrictions and guilt.

Betty Friedan

20th-century American political activist

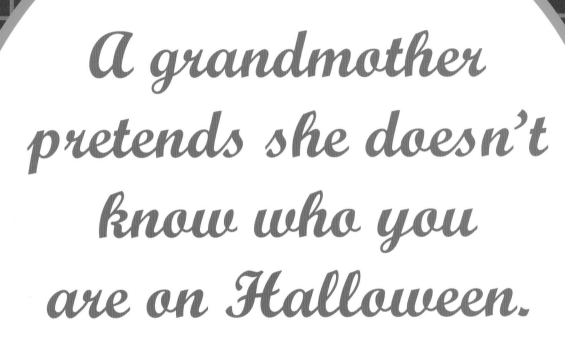

A grandmother pretends she doesn't know who you are on Halloween.

Erma Bombeck (1927–1996)

American writer

Holding these babies in my arms makes me realize the miracle my husband and I began.

Betty Ford, b. 1918

American First Lady

Photography Credits